a gift for

from

A Couple's FIRST YEAR Devotions

Abingdon Press

Nashville

A Couple's First Year

This book is printed on acid-free paper.

ISBN 978-1-4267-4816-5

With contributions from:
Amy Valdez Barker and Richard Barker II
Lloyd and Clare Doyle
Tim and Becky Eberhart
Warren and Mary Ebinger
Kel and Ellen Groseclose
James Chongho and Karen Eunsook Kim
Bill and Katie Treadway
John and Ginny Underwood

12 13 14 15 16 17 18 19 20 21—10 9 8 7 6 5 4 3 2 1
MANUFACTURED IN THE UNITED STATES OF AMERICA

We are more likely to be blessings to others when we feel good about ourselves. We also tend to notice each other's shortcomings more frequently when we're struggling with our own problems. If we're going to bless others, and especially our spouses, we must first come to terms with ourselves. Before we're able to share peace, we must experience it personally. When we find fault with people around us, it probably means we need to do some good old-fashioned soul searching.

Continue encouraging each other and building each other up, just like you are doing already.

—*1 Thessalonians 5:11*

Taste and see

how good the LORD is!

–Psalm 34:8

There are different spiritual gifts
but the same Spirit . . . and there are
different activities but the same God
who produces all of them in everyone.
    –1 Corinthians 12:4-6

$\mathcal{A}$ bouquet of roses from the garden, with their beauty and fragrance, goes a long way toward solving arguments. The sound of gentle words such as "I'm sorry" or "I love you" can soften even the hardest hearts. Holding hands while going for a walk employs all our human senses, especially if you tuck a bit of food in your pocket. Tangible expressions of caring both connect us to God and bring us together as a couple.

In a marriage, one may be a morning person; the other definitely not. One turns the thermostat up; the other turns it down. One knows the precise bank balance; the other's not even sure where the bank is. The important thing is to see these differences as a source of strength and joy. God has gone to considerable effort to make each of us unique. The least we can do is honor that.

$\mathcal{L}$ife is lived in the realm of "everyday." It's where work is done, tears are wiped, laughter is heard, and love is shared. It's where hearts are broken and mended. In marriage, it's what starts when the honeymoon is over. The goal is not merely to survive but to prosper, to find meaning and joy in each moment. We need to plan for the future yet live in the present. It's a delicate balancing act requiring God's constant guidance.

Remember this day. . . .

–*Exodus 13:3*

We want our lives to count for something. Jesus teaches that we win not by gaining but by giving, not by standing up but by stepping down. Pretending to be something we aren't or trying to camouflage our limitations doesn't cut it when it comes to God. Once we've learned to accept ourselves as we are—weaknesses and strengths, irritating and lovely habits alike—we've taken a giant step toward making our lives count for plenty. That's a necessary prelude for receiving and using the gifts God has given us.

The one who is greatest among you will be your servant. All who lift themselves up will be brought low. But all who make themselves low will be lifted up.

—*Matthew 23:11-12*

elationships go better when partners criticize less and do their own "knitting"—that is, take care of their own daily duties. To nag those closest to us is counterproductive, always. We all experience frequent lapses. After all, we are human. When the relationship gets balled up, don't wait until it's hopelessly tangled. Attend to the problem, then get on knitting your lives together with God and each another. You'll end up with a beautiful tapestry of love.

Each of us will give an account of ourselves to God. So stop judging each other.

–Romans 14:12-13a

One night he asked her, "What was the happiest part of today?"

"I was angry most of the day. I can't think of anything," she replied irritably.

"I know, but this morning we saw tiny green tomatoes in our garden and the bright yellow and purple pansies."

"I liked that," she admitted, "and when you suggested fast food after my busy day at work."

No matter what type of day we have, there is always something good if we try to find it.

A joyful heart
brightens one's face,
but a troubled heart
breaks the spirit.
—Proverbs 15:13

S ome things are best when they're fresh: carrots just dug from the garden, chocolate chip cookies still warm from the oven, coffee brewed moments before the first sip. But far better than these is God's steadfast love and mercy, which are new every day. As the sun rises faithfully each morning, so does God's grace, all fresh and pure, delivered right to our doorstep.

Certainly the faithful love of the LORD hasn't ended; certainly God's compassion isn't through! They are renewed every morning. Great is your faithfulness. —Lamentations 3:22-23

Complimenting your spouse is the best "reward" you can give for what he or she does. We easily give compliments to those with whom we work, to our neighbors, and to friends; yet often we take those closest to us for granted. One way to change this pattern is to think of at least one thing each day you can say in a complimentary way to your partner. Compliment your spouse face-to-face, offering a hug or kiss afterward, which is like icing on the cake.

Her husband praises her. —Proverbs 21:28

Brothers and sisters, I myself don't think I've

reached it, but I do this one thing: I forget

about the things behind me and reach out for

the things ahead of me. The goal I pursue is

the prize of God's upward call in Christ Jesus.

—Philippians 3:13–14

Sometimes we carry unkind words or hurt feelings from the past into the present. It's like excess baggage. This can make us heavy in heart and mind. Just as the apostle Paul recognized that he had to let go of his past (which was not very pleasant to recall), so also must we. We must recognize unhappy experiences for what they were, and then let them go. Too much awaits you today and tomorrow to let the past cloud the sky of the future.

*S*haring food brings you together. It may be soup and sandwiches at home for lunch, a carefully packed picnic lunch in the park, an inexpensive meal from a drive-in on a busy night, a romantic candlelit dinner prepared at home, or a beautiful expensive restaurant. It matters not. What does matter is that you enjoy the food and share together the events of the day, or words of love in between the simplest of food, and know this is a time to cherish together.

JESUS SAID TO THEM,

"COME AND HAVE BREAKFAST."

—*John 21:12*

Be kind,

compassionate, and

forgiving to each

other, in the same

way God forgave

you in Christ.

—Ephesians 4:32

"*I*'m sorry": there are no more important words in a marriage. They can be hard words to say, however, because of feelings that keep us from recognizing some fault we have—from wanting one's own way to saying words that hurt deeply. Being sorry, however, is not merely saying two words. It is doing something about the wrong. It is making it right, if possible, or determining not to repeat it.

*D*o you ever wonder if there's really enough time for everything that has to be done? Many couples are caught in a time bind that seems to allow no opportunity to really talk together except about immediate concerns of the day. What can we do about it? Even those couples who lead the busiest lives somehow find time to talk together, if they see this as a high priority. The key to finding the time is in your hands, and it can open new doors to understanding and love.

There's a season for everything and a time for every matter

under the heavens.

—*Ecclesiastes 3:1*

*T*aking ourselves too seriously diminishes the joy and fun of marriage. There may be serious concerns that face us, some with deadlines; yet there is such a need for laughter in the midst of everything else—often as a release of the tensions of the day. Laughter has been called "good medicine for the soul." Joy and laughter are closely intertwined. Weeping may bind us together, too, but laughter sets us free, for the moment, from sadness.

*F*or better, for worse; in sickness and in health—these words were part of your wedding vows. Every marriage has its share of sadness, whether it's in relation to grieving the loss of parents or others, moving, saying goodbye to friends, or dealing with sickness or other hardships. Joy and sorrow are part of every life. You need a strong marriage in order to share both the happy and the sad times.

Jesus began to cry.

—John 11:35

*S*trength can mean many things. It can be a show of power, a measurement of influence or material value, or an advantage over another in a relationship. Scripture, however, refers to a different kind of strength. True strength is to humble yourself before God. It's to take control of your emotions and allow your faith to lead you. It's finding the patience to listen for the answers in God's time, not our own.

Better to be patient than a warrior, and better to have self-control than to capture a city.
—Proverbs 16:32

She wants chocolate and flowers every so often. He wants time in his lounge chair to watch sports. She wants to drive to the mountains, and he wants to hit the beach. We have different ways of relaxing and different ways of wanting to nurture ourselves and our relationship. That is the key. We must nurture our relationship. It will not just happen. We have to take time and be together and continue to rekindle the fire of our love. If we don't, it can go out, and we'll wonder what happened.

In your presence is total celebration.
Beautiful things are always in your right hand.
–Psalm 16:11

No one pours new wine into old leather wineskins; otherwise, the wine would burst the wineskins and the wine would be lost and the wineskins destroyed. But new wine is for new wineskins.

–Mark 2:22

The families we grow up in have many similarities and yet many differences. When we get married, we can't do everything the way her family or his family did. We have to find a new way. Some traditions we can keep, others have to be blended, and new ones need to be created. That's how it works in marriage. We become a new family, and we have to begin afresh. We have to begin our own traditions. We have to form our own way of doing things.

God created this world—and what a glorious place it is! As a couple, we can experience the glory of God's creation by enjoying it together. One couple goes camping and enjoys seeing many different places. One couple travels the globe. One couple likes to sip coffee each morning on their patio. Another likes to enjoy their houseplants. But all experience God's presence in their lives as they share spectacular and ordinary moments in nature with their spouse.

I raise my eyes toward the mountains.
Where will my help come from?
My help comes from the LORD,
the maker of heaven and earth.

—Psalm 121:1-2

*D*ate night may sound extravagant and impossible to some couples, but it is an excellent and necessary way to stay in touch. Think about the time you spent together before you were married—how exciting and wonderful it was simply to be together. You might say, "We're together anyway; why bother?" But it's not the same. Now that you're married you still need to plan for regular "special times" together—times when you may focus only on each other. It takes intentional effort to keep your relationship strong.

"Everybody who hears these words of mine and puts them into practice is like a wise builder who built a house on bedrock. The rain fell, the floods came, and the wind blew and beat against that house. It didn't fall because it was firmly set on bedrock." —*Matthew 7:24-25*

*L*ove is the "salt" of marriage. How can we have a marriage if the love is gone? We have to work on keeping love and our relationship alive. It is so important to keep the love in marriage. And let's face it: sometimes it is hard, for all of us have quirks. Some like to flip television channels, some don't clean up after themselves, some snore, and others overeat. We can overlook our spouse's quirks because of our love for each other. But that takes work.

You are the salt of the earth. But if salt loses its saltiness, how will it become salty again?
—*Matthew 5:13*

I know the plans I have in mind for you, declares the LORD; they are plans for peace, not disaster, to give you a future filled with hope.

—Jeremiah 29:11

God wants us to have a good and successful future. God cares about every last hair on our head. God cares about us. Of course we do live in a broken world where there is suffering and pain. But with God's help, we can get through the suffering. If we take time to have fun together and build memories together, then we will have the staying power to get through the more difficult times. What a wonderful promise we have that God wants us to have a future of hope.

*M*arriage is about give and take. There is a lot of compromise. She likes to flip the television button; he likes to watch the news. But they want to spend time together, so they compromise. She flips through the news stations, and around and back, and he catches the news in bits and pieces. If we don't nurture our marriage, it will, like the plants, wither and die. If we become so focused on what I want or how I want to spend time, we draw further and further apart.

When the sun came up, it scorched the plants; and they dried up because they had no roots.

—*Mark 4:6*

*Y*ou can live happily ever after, not as the fairytales say, but as a real couple journeying through life under God's grace. There is no foolproof guarantee for a successful marriage. But if you unconditionally love each other, nurture your marriage, and seek Christ's guidance, you have a solid foundation for God-given happiness together. Marriage takes time, effort, and energy. Keep on nurturing your marriage, and may the peace of God-in-Christ be yours.

May there be peace with the brothers and sisters as well as love with the faith that comes from God the Father and the Lord Jesus Christ. —*Ephesians 6:23*

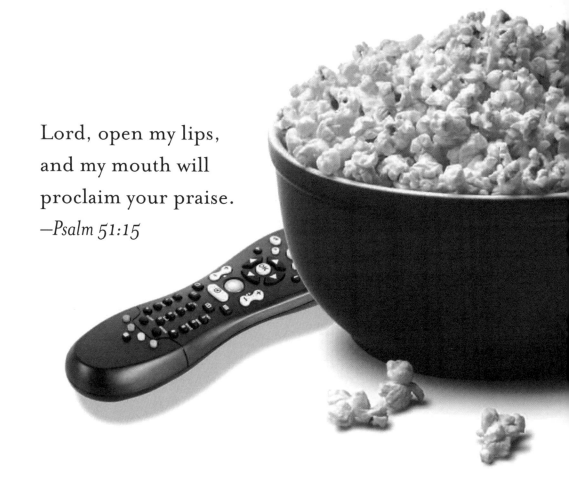

Lord, open my lips,
and my mouth will
proclaim your praise.
—*Psalm 51:15*

*H*ow we all love to watch movies. Not only do we laugh, cry, and cheer while we're watching them, but when we recall watching them together we get to experience the fun we had all over again. In the beginning, you created your marriage. You created it by committing to each other. But you have to daily re-create your marriage. What better way than through recreation together. It is so important to have fun together and to laugh together, to learn together and to grow together.

The LORD detests
the path of the wicked,
but loves those who
pursue righteousness.

—Proverbs 15:9

$\mathcal{W}$e all gain perspective about relationships and marriage from our parents. Communication, affection, trust, compromise, and sacrifice are all necessary ingredients for a successful marriage. Try to evaluate perceived mistakes, looking at the cause and effects in order to gain a true understanding of the situation. If you are able to obtain that understanding, then you are less likely to repeat the mistake. A mistake is only destructive when it is repeated and nothing is gained or learned. Handled appropriately, a mistake is actually an opportunity for growth.

*I*t seems we spend Sunday nights making sure we're ready for the week, and the next minute we look up and it's Friday afternoon. Where does the time go? If we don't make time to live a little in between the monotony, we may wake up and find that our lives have passed us by. God has created this beautiful world for us to enjoy. There's a lot more to life than what's between point A and point B. Make every minute count this week.

$\mathcal{T}$hink about the things above and not things on earth. —*Colossians 3:2*

$\mathcal{T}$he seed that fell on good soil are those who hear the word and commit themselves to it with a good and upright heart. Through their resolve, they bear fruit. —*Luke 8:15*

People often tell lies because they are afraid of the consequences of telling the truth. We are very good at masking ourselves outwardly and lying to ourselves inwardly. Yet God sees through the deception. We need to understand that being honest allows us to lay our burdens down. Honesty has the ability to free our spirits. Honesty is the key to all our relationships, but most especially with our spouse. Look for opportunities to build and grow through honest conversations.

$\mathcal{W}$e live in such a "now" culture. We have technology that allows us to use our time more efficiently, yet we still don't have enough time to do everything we want to in any given day. God would not have us sit idle, but we must have faith that God will open doors for us in God's own time. Patience is kind and nurturing; it listens, it teaches, it guides, it leads by example, and it waits for direction.

$\mathcal{A}$fter all, you know that the testing of your faith produces endurance. —*James 1:3*

For every breath we take, for every kiss we give, for every hug we offer or receive, for every meal we eat, we have our heavenly Father to thank. God gives us so many blessings and gifts that every day should be like a birthday party. Being thankful helps you appreciate all your gifts. The more thankful you become about everything, the more blessings you are able to see. Thankfulness enriches your life.

*S*cripture tells us that Peter began to sink when he took his eyes off of Jesus. Peter allowed the troubles around him to take his focus off of God. We face troubled waters every day—in our work, in our community, and even in our marriage. What we have to realize is that, like Peter, if we want to wade through the water successfully, we have to keep our focus on Jesus. If we do, all the troubles will take care of themselves.

He said to them, "Why are you afraid, you people of weak faith?" Then he got up and gave orders to the winds and the lake, and there was a great calm. – *Matthew 8:26*

*S*ometimes our focus is on where the next paycheck is coming from, how many bills we have to pay, and what we deem "valuable." We argue about who makes more money, why we think we don't have enough money, and why we need to give to this or that cause. God reminds us that it isn't what we have or what we do that will delight our souls. Why do we get caught up in the pursuit of material things? Can they enhance our relationship?

$\mathcal{W}$hy spend money for
what isn't food, and your
earnings for what doesn't
satisfy? Listen carefully to
me and eat what is good;
enjoy the richest of feasts.

– *Isaiah 55:2*

*W*isdom is better

than pearls;

nothing is more

delightful than she.

– *Proverbs 8:11*

$\mathcal{W}$e humans value success. By our measurements, a person is successful

if he or she gains wealth, influence, power, and prestige. Scripture says,

however, that there is another kind of success: succeeding God's way.

Regardless of the conditions we may live in, we have succeeded in

life because we have one another. We have joy and laughter.

We have happiness and contentment. We have faith

and, above all, love. This is success God's way.

*B*eing married helps us with doing right, rather than doing what is easy. At times we may want to just give up honest values and take the easy, crooked road. Thankfully, we have each other; we can encourage one another, looking to the other to help make our paths straight. It's not always easy to take the right path, but with the help of God and each other, we can do it.

*P*repare the way for the Lord; make his paths straight. . . . The crooked will be made straight and the rough places made smooth.

— *Luke 3:4-5*

$\mathcal{W}$hoever is faithful with little

is also faithful with much. – *Luke 16:10*

*T*rust is a major part of any relationship, especially a marriage. Always telling the truth is a very hard thing for some people to get used to. Often people are too scared to suffer the consequences of something they have done, so they lie. Scripture reminds us that we have to be trustworthy partners in our relationship. This allows us to take advantage of the true riches that trust can give. Trust frees us to accept each other for who we truthfully are.

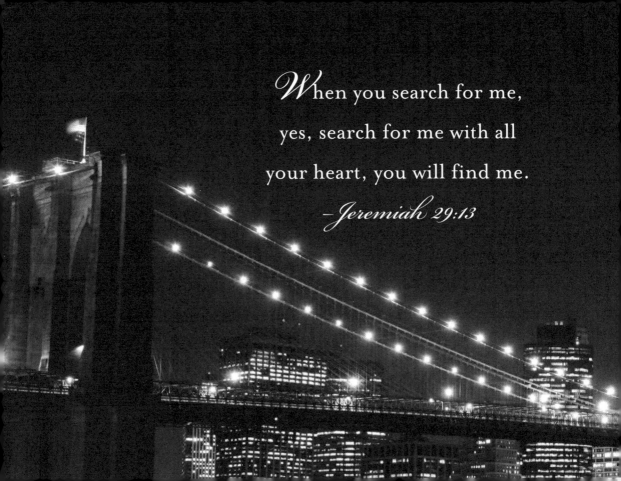

*W*hen you search for me,

yes, search for me with all

your heart, you will find me.

– Jeremiah 29:13

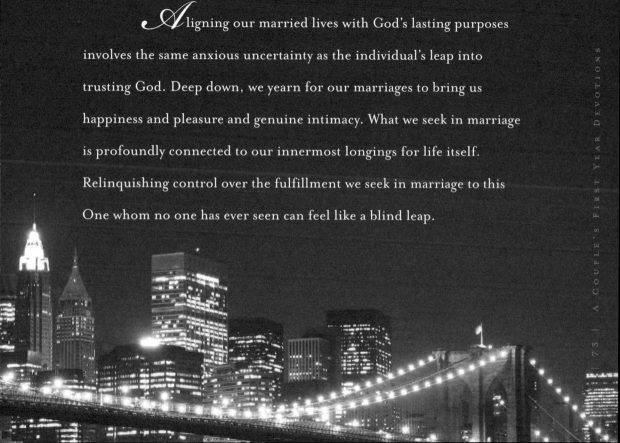

*A*ligning our married lives with God's lasting purposes involves the same anxious uncertainty as the individual's leap into trusting God. Deep down, we yearn for our marriages to bring us happiness and pleasure and genuine intimacy. What we seek in marriage is profoundly connected to our innermost longings for life itself. Relinquishing control over the fulfillment we seek in marriage to this One whom no one has ever seen can feel like a blind leap.

This is my prayer: that your

love might become even more

and more rich with knowledge

and all kinds of insight.

–Philippians 1:9

*I*n a marriage that seeks to serve Christ, the way of love will be the foundation upon which husband and wife unite, relate, communicate, and plan. God's purposes become our plans when the love we know in Christ becomes our lasting guide. This kind of love is God's answer in Christ to our confusion of purpose and direction; it has the power to make us pure, and in it rests our hope for life eternal.

*T*hen God said, "Let us make

humanity in our image. . . ."

God created humanity in God's

own image, in the divine image

God created them, male and

female God created them.

—Genesis 1:26–27

$\mathcal{W}$e do not exist as solitary selves, but in, through, and because of relationship. And as we grow deeper into the life of God, we find that God is ultimately not present in the solitude of our individual selves but in the space between. And where does love abide if not in the space between? To be in loving relationship—most especially the relationship of marriage—is to be in the image of God.

Our differences as husband and wife are not problems but possibilities. That one is gifted here and another there need not be the basis for fighting but the probability of a broader vision for both. Together we are smarter, more capable, and ultimately more complete. Marriage, grounded in love, is where our unique selves can be both given and received and thus made whole.

*S*erve each other according to the gift each person has received, as good managers of God's diverse gifts. *–1 Peter 4:10*

*I*n marriage, husband and wife unite to become what the Bible calls "one flesh" (Matthew 19:6). Two persons with separate hearts and minds intentionally join to form a new person with one heart and mind. Maybe a more accurate description is that in marriage, two become three, so that we are husband, wife, and the One who is our relationship. Regardless of how you add it up, being truly married means the two-in-one relationship has become more important than the single self.

Now I encourage you, brothers and sisters, in the name of our Lord Jesus Christ: agree with each other and . . . be restored with the same mind and the same purpose. *–1 Corinthians 1:10*

*S*tewardship of marriage involves using the goodness generated by our loving relationship for the good of others. Because God is Lord over all and the giver of all things, including our marriage, and because Christ has shown us the way, Christian marriage does not exist solely for the self-contained enjoyment of husband and wife but as a gift to the world. From God, to us, for others: the simple, eternal design.

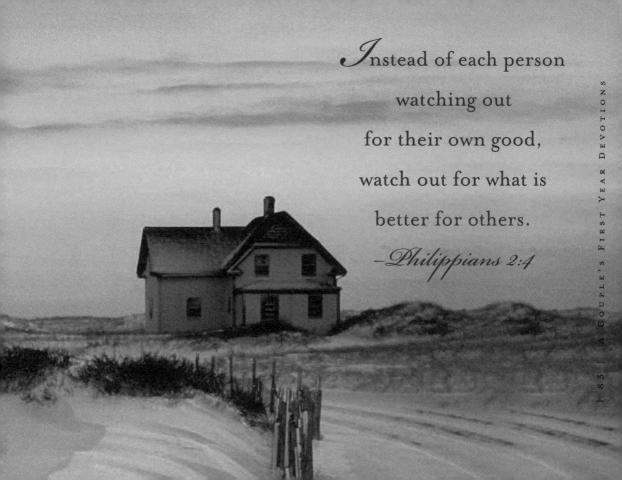

*I*nstead of each person

watching out

for their own good,

watch out for what is

better for others.

–Philippians 2:4

*T*wo are better than one because they have

a good return for their hard work.

If either should fall, one can pick up the other.

—Ecclesiastes 4:9-10

*G*od does not point us anywhere without providing a way; and in the experience of a loving relationship, we see the divine mind providing one of the more beautiful of ways. Marriage can be a means of grace in which those things we can't do as one alone become possible as two together. God gives us relationship and the capacity to transform one another by encouragement, support, and love.

*G*od saw everything he had made: it was supremely good.

–Genesis 1:31

There are good times and bad times. At times we love, and at times we argue and fight. That is why it is so important for us to always return to our Sender who said, "It was supremely good." It was very good when we got married. It was very good in the beginning of all things. Reminding ourselves that it was God who made us come together in the first place always helps us be more mindful of God's original blessing.

Love is patient, love is kind, it isn't jealous, it doesn't brag, it isn't arrogant, it isn't rude, it doesn't seek its own advantage, it isn't irritable, it doesn't keep a record of complaints.
—*1 Corinthians 13:4-5*

*T*he *A* of love is *accept*—accepting a spouse as he or she is. The first rule of happiness is accepting each other. The *B* of love is *believe*. And the *C* of love is *care*. Believing in and caring for each other helps us through our everyday trials. The *D* of love is *desire*—in other words, expecting each other to become the best we can be. The *E* of love is *erase*— forgiving and forgetting each other's wrongdoings and shortcomings.

*O*ur marriages need regular "health checkups." Living in the same house under the same roof doesn't necessarily make a house a home. Because we tend to take each other for granted, we often fail to see each other's wounds and hurts. Unfortunately, we're often more compassionate toward "outsiders" than we are toward our own spouses. And yet, unless we learn to be kind and compassionate to each other at home, forgiving each other, we will never fully discover our ability to love others.

Live your life with love, following the example of Christ, who loved us and gave himself for us.

—Ephesians 5:2a

*L*ove is telling your wife or husband, "You are beautiful."
God made us lovable by loving us first. This is why we are beautiful. And
by telling our spouses that they are beautiful, they will become beautiful.
Try it! We are beautiful because we are loved by God. And that's what
makes us beautiful to each other. Have you said, "You're beautiful" lately?
Remember, everyone needs to hear the words "You are beautiful."

Rise up, my dearest,

my fairest, and go.

–Song of Songs 2:13

Here, the winter is past; the rains have come and gone. Blossoms have appeared in the land; the season of singing has arrived, and the sound of the turtledove is heard in our land.

–Song of Songs 2:11-12

Love is helping our spouses experience the fullness of God's blessing in the world. Love is reminding each other that the winter is past, the rains are over and gone. Most of us do better in an encouraging environment. When we encourage our spouses, we help them see themselves the way God sees them. Love encourages the other person to make the best of their God-given talent.

*L*ife is a journey. Marriage is taking that journey together, not knowing what's ahead. This can make life challenging and chaotic at times. Sometimes we ask ourselves, *Would I have done this if I had known then what it would be like?* Yet life is not a dress rehearsal; it is a live show. We just have to learn as we go along. Don't expect your husband or your wife to know everything. We are all students of life, especially when it comes to loving someone.

$\mathcal{Y}$ou were called to this kind of endurance, because Christ suffered on your behalf. He left you an example so that you might follow in his footsteps. —*1 Peter 2:21*